17 YEARS WANDERING AMONG THE ABORIGINALS

A man, his two wives, and son outside their bark home.
The adults have cord necklaces, one wife has a cord band
over her right chest, and the man also has a cord arm band.
Note the horizontal chest and abdominal scars applied
to the man and the small vertical scars above the breasts
of the central female. Cardwell, north of Townsville.
(Atkinson collection, c 1890s.)

17 YEARS WANDERING AMONG THE ABORIGINALS

James Morrill 1864

With photographs published
by Eric Mjoberg 1918

Published by David M. Welch 2006.
Australian Aboriginal Culture Series No. 1

17 Years Wandering Among the Aboriginals.

New 2006 edition, containing James Morrill's original 1864 text, with accompanying photographs previously published by Eric Mjoberg in 1918. This includes photographs by Alfred Atkinson and James Handley, taken about the 1890s.

Published by David M. Welch
Box 503, CMB 19
Virginia
Northern Territory. 0822
Australia.
Fax (61)(8)8983 1145
www.aboriginalculture.com.au

Australian Aboriginal Culture Series No.1

National Library of Australia
Cataloguing-in-Publication entry:

Morrill, James, 1824-1865
17 years wandering among the Aboriginals.
New ed.
ISBN 0 9775035 0 X

1. Morrill, James, 1824-1865. 2. Aboriginal Australians - Queensland - Social life and customs - 19th century. 3. Castaways - Queensland. I. Mjoberg, Eric, 1882-1938. II Title.

305.8991509943

Typeset in Indesign, 11.5 point Garamond, and graphic design by Jane Kerkmann.
Printed on Matt Art 130gsm paper, section sewn.
Printed by Custom Press Pty Ltd., South Australia.

Cover photographs:
Group of northern men and women with painted rainforest shields, spears, boomerangs and large battle sword-clubs. The men have multiple horizontal cicatrices (scars) over their chests and abdomens, and two have feather headdresses. Some women wear necklaces, and one man wears a pearlshell pendant. European clothing has been introduced. Northern Queensland. (Atkinson collection, c 1890s.)
Headdress made from feathers, wood, beeswax resin and red abrus seeds. (Welch collection.)

SKETCH OF A RESIDENCE

AMONG THE

ABORIGINALS

OF

NORTHERN QUEENSLAND

FOR

SEVENTEEN YEARS

BEING A NARRATIVE OF MY LIFE, SHIPWRECK, LANDING, ON THE COAST, RESIDENCE AMONG THE ABORIGINALS, WITH AN ACCOUNT OF THEIR MANNERS AND CUSTOMS, AND MODE OF LIVING.

TOGETHER WITH

NOTICES OF MANY OF THE NATURAL PRODUCTIONS, AND OF THE NATURE OF THE COUNTRY

BY

JAMES MORRILL

A native of Abridge, near Maldon, Essex.

BOSTON

PRINTED AT NEWCOMB'S STEAM PRINTING OFFICES, THREADNEEDLE STREET, 1864

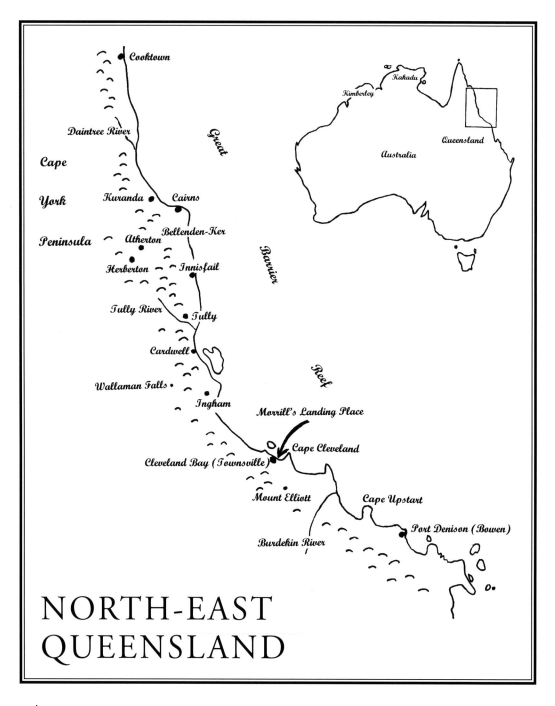

NORTH-EAST
QUEENSLAND

Cooktown

Daintree River

Great

Cape

York

Kuranda • Cairns

Peninsula

Bellenden-Ker

Atherton

Herberton   Innisfail

Barrier

Tully River   Tully

Cardwell

Reef

Wallaman Falls •

Ingham

Morrill's Landing Place

Cape Cleveland

Cleveland Bay (Townsville)

Mount Elliott

Cape Upstart

Port Denison (Bowen)

Burdekin River

Kimberley   Kakadu

Queensland

Australia

CONTENTS

CHAPTER 1   Page 6

Birth and parentage – Education – Choice of profession – Apprenticeship – My first long voyage in the *Ramalees* – Voyage to New Zealand and back – Shipped on board the *Peruvian*.

CHAPTER 2   Page 10

Voyage from Sydney to China – Shipwreck – 42 days on the raft – Reaching the land – Kind reception by the natives – Death of Mr. Wilmott and a seaman – Life among the natives – Death of the apprentice boy, the captain, and his wife – Restoration to civilized life.

CHAPTER 3   Page 52

The Aboriginals – Nomadic habits – Living in tribes – What they eat as food – Language – How the natives make fire – The ceremony of making the lads men – Relationship – How they dispose of the dead – Flax grown and the uses they make of it – Description of the Country – Gold – Extinction of the race – Appeal for the natives.

POSTSCRIPT   Page 72

Wood engraving of
James Morrill,
by Samuel Calvert
(1828-1913), from an
illustrated newspaper.
National Library of Australia.
nla.pic-an9885580.

Eric Mjoberg's simple
camp with a cover made
from folded bark in the
Aboriginal style, at the
Coleman River,
Cape York Peninsula.
To the right is his camera,
on its stand, which he
carried everywhere.

introduction
INTRODUCTION

This book is a combination of the true account by shipwrecked sailor, James Morrill, written in 1864, and the rare photographs published in 1918 by Swedish naturalist, Eric Mjoberg, both describing Aborigines in the Queensland region of Australia.

JAMES MORRILL (1824-1865)

In 1846 James Morrill was shipwrecked on Horseshoe Reef or the Minerva Shoal in the Pacific Ocean. The crew made a raft which floated over 900k westward, crossed the Great Barrier Reef, the longest coral reef in the world, and eventually landed on the Queensland coast of north east Australia, at what became the southern point of Cleveland Bay, near Townsville. He then lived for 17 years with Aborigines in the Townsville-Bowen region, the only white person in that part of Australia, until the spread of colonisation north from Sydney finally found him. Morrill's story, though brief, gives insight into Aboriginal day to day society untouched by European civilisation, and his account was published as a pamphlet and in newspapers in 1864.

Known as "Jimmy" or "Jemmy" to his friends, Morrill's surname is sometimes spelt "Morrell" or "Murrells". After 17 years of isolation from his own people, he remembered his name as "Morrill" and this is the spelling on his original publication and his gravestone. Later, it was learned that the correct spelling of his ancestors in England was "Murrells" and he was, in fact, born "James Murrells" in England.

Following his return to civilisation, he assisted both Aboriginal people and European settlers in understanding each other in that region, but he died two years later, and most Australian people today are unaware of his story. The Bowen Historical Society has re-published his story in 1964 as *The Story of*

Portrait of
James Morrill
taken by Wilder, a
photographer from
Rockhampton,
Queensland.
(Collection:
John Oxley Library,
State Library of
Queensland.
Image No. 14463)

James Morrill, and again as *James Morrill, his life and adventures* in 2002, and these contain more background information on him.

ERIC MJOBERG (1882-1938)

Eric Mjoberg was a Swedish naturalist who made two scientific expeditions to Australia and recorded its flora, fauna, geography and people in 1910-1911 and 1912-1913. He was the first Swedish explorer to use a camera for cinematographic (motion picture) film and the second Swedish explorer, after Daniel Solander, to visit Australia.

Mjoberg wrote two books on Australia, *Bland Vilda Djur Och Folk I Australien* (*Among Wild Animals and People in Australia*) in 1915, and *Bland Stenaldersmanniskor I Queenslands Vildmarker* (*Among Stone Age People in Queensland's Wilderness*) in 1918. Most of the photographs in Mjoberg's book on Queensland were taken by himself, and the one here on page viii shows his simple camp made for him by the Aborigines, with one of his cameras on a tripod.

In the introduction to his Queensland book, he acknowledges assistance from Captain Fry, the Queensland state photographer, in giving him some photographs, but it is not clear as to which photos. Mjoberg also states that a few photos are from other sources, and he acknowledges the occasional photo of an animal taken in a state zoo.

However, research reveals that Mjoberg's clearest photographs of Aboriginal people were taken by Cairns photographer Alfred Atkinson (1867-1950), or Atkinson's partner, James Handley (died 1900), probably in the 1890s. These are identified here in this book with the annotation: "Atkinson collection, c 1890s". Cairns was established in 1876, and James Handley had a photographic studio there, when Atkinson joined him in 1890 or soon after. The colonisation and development of the region, and the displacement and modernisation of Aboriginal people was rapid, with the building of the Kuranda railway in 1886.

This rare collection of photographs of life in north Queensland, compiled by Eric Mjoberg, is reproduced here, and includes many images of people and places from the region between Cairns and Townsville, just north of where James Morrill spent his time living with the Aborigines fifty to sixty years earlier.

Many aspects of Aboriginal culture are not uniform throughout Australia, but vary from region to region, influenced by local climate, vegetation, resources, and local custom. Some of the Aboriginal beliefs and practices described in the text did not apply to people living in other regions of Australia. Similarly, some of the items seen in the accompanying photographs are unique to northern Queensland. Items such as the large rainforest shields, large wooden sword-clubs and outrigger canoes depicted here are used in the Cape York Peninsula region of north Queensland, and may not have been seen by Morrill, who lived mainly in the area south of Townsville.

The text of each caption accompanying the illustrations here is a combination of the original text by Mjoberg and further descriptive notes I have added. Aboriginal people were regarded as being so different to Europeans that words used to describe the people, such as "blacks", "savages", and "half-civilised" were standard terminology for the time, and these terms are retained in some of the text captions, for historical accuracy.

I would like to thank Erika Sundquist of Sundborn and Inger Ekenberg of Helsingborg for translating parts of the original Swedish Mjoberg text, Ann Wills and the Bowen Historical Society for providing material they had available on James Morrill, and Pat Broughton and the Cairns Historical Society for providing additional information on Eric Mjoberg and Alfred Atkinson, and for identifying nineteen of the photographs here as being from the Atkinson Collection. The Cairns Historical Society also holds the original

Atkinson Collection glass plates. I would also like to thank Peter Bridge of Perth for making me aware of James Morrill's story and Grant Husband of Darwin for making me aware of Mjoberg's original books. The John Oxley Library and National Library of Australia supplied images of Morrill, and initial research was done at the Battye Library (State Library of Western Australia) where copies were made of the 1863 South Australian Advertiser containing parts of Morrill's initial account.

David M. Welch, Publisher. 2006

Men and boys with ceremonial body paint, prepared for a coroboree. The man at far left wears a headband with shell pendant over his forehead, nose bone, a large pearlshell pendant from his neck, and a European brass buckle belt. Other men wear nose bones and hold shields, spears, long sword-clubs and a boomerang. (Atkinson collection, c. 1890s.)

The Advertiser.

ADELAIDE: TUESDAY, OCTOBER 6, 1863.

A SHORT TIME ago we received from our telegraphic reporter in Victoria a short but very striking account of a European who had been discovered amongst the aboriginals of the Queensland district, after living with them for many years, and becoming to a great extent naturalized to their habits. More recently a pamphlet has found its way into our hands written by the individual referred to, and containing so graphic an account of his adventures that we have great pleasure in laying the substance of it before our readers. It will, in its quaint style of narrative remind many of that charming book of their childhood, Robinson Crusoe. It opens as follows :—

"I, James Morrill, was born on the 20th May, 1824, in the parish of Abridge, near Maldon, in the county of Essex, where my mother and father where also brought up from childhood before me. My father was a millwright and engineer by profession, and carried on his business in Swan Yard, in connection with an uncle of mine (James Hays). I had one brother, older than myself, and three sisters, who were younger. When old enough I was sent to the national school in the village; an old soldier was the schoolmaster, Mr. George Bridge, who, among other things, taught us the manual exercise, and frequently put us through our facings. Nothing particularly marked my school course worth mentioning; I was

book, Bible, and hymn-book." ...cook, a Prayer-

The story then proceeds at some length to relate many curious circumstances in reference to the aboriginals of the district, in which fear, curiosity, and wonder are strangely blended. In these details a long period seems to have been absorbed ; in fact, the author of the story scarcely knows how long. All he can say is, "time ran on ;" but whether "time" is to be measured by months or years he does not tell us. It is, however, pretty clear that a lengthened period is intended, and many romantic and harrowing incidents occurred in the meanwhile. About three years prior to his deliverance Morrill heard that a white man had been seen in that part of the country, and he not unnaturally conceived the idea of getting away from his aboriginal friends. Afterwards other reports came in, and Morrill gleaned from the description of the natives that white men were undoubtedly on that part of the continent. It is an unhappy circumstance that his first knowledge of the contiguity of white men was derived from the reports that numbers of the aboriginals had been shot dead by their strange visitors. When in the neighborhood of the Burdekin River, Morrill says :—

"I received almost daily reports of the white people. There were two....

James Morrill's account as it was reported around Australia at the time:
The South Australian Advertiser, Tuesday October 6, 1863.

CHAPTER 1

BIRTH AND PARENTAGE – EDUCATION
CHOICE OF PROFESSION – APPRENTICESHIP
MY FIRST LONG VOYAGE IN THE *RAMALEES*
VOYAGE TO NEW ZEALAND AND BACK
SHIPPED ON BOARD THE *PERUVIAN*

I, James Morrill, was born on the 20th May, 1824, in the parish of Abridge, near Maldon, in the county of Essex, where my father and mother were also brought up from childhood before me. My father was a millwright and engineer by profession, and carried on his business in Swan Yard, in connection with one of my uncles (James Hays). I had one brother older than myself, and three sisters, who were younger. When old enough, I was sent to the National School in the village. Mr. George Bridge, an old soldier, was the schoolmaster, who, among other things, taught us the manual exercise, and frequently put us through our facings. Nothing worth mentioning marked my school course. I was as often as most boys of my age ready for a fight or a game.

When I was about 13 or 14 years of age, and had acquired an ordinary education, such as was generally given in those days, and was old enough to be of use, I went with my brother, to work in my father's shop. But I was of rather a restless disposition, the workshop was too confining for me, I was always glad of an opportunity to get away from it, if only for a day; I was particularly pleased if I could get among the shipping, the facility for which was great, as we lived so near the coast town, and so many small craft used to come up the River Blackwater, close to where I lived. Among the friends who visited my father's house was Mr. James Firman, a pilot, who used to pilot the craft down the Blackwater River, at Maldon; I frequently went with him in the

Parts of coastal Queensland are characterised by flat plains and large rivers against a backdrop of rainforest mountains. Cairns.

vessels he used to pilot out, and return with him in the pilot boat. Of course, I was only allowed to go in fine weather; the fine white sails and the beautiful sea quite charmed me – I was always wishing I could be a sailor – which I made no secret of. My father and mother often told me that I should be glad to be at home again, which I found true enough in my after experience.

On one of those trips with the pilot, the captain seeing me a smart lad, enquired who I was, and asked the pilot whether I should like to go to sea, to which he replied that was just what I had wanted to do for some time. He asked me if I would go with him, and on promising to buy me clothes and what other articles I wanted, in Shields, the place where he was bound for, I was only too willing to go. So without consulting my father and mother, away I went on my first voyage, in the brig *Royal Sailor*, belonging to the Maldon Shipping Company.

Barron Falls, near Cairns, in the Wet Season (November to April). Enormous volumes of water pass through a narrow gorge and then open out into a wide stream.

The captain was a very good man, he was a Wesleyan, and when on shore a local preacher of that body. Every night at eight o'clock, weather permitting, he used to call all hands together and read the bible to us, afterwards we sang a hymn, and he used to read prayers. He was a very kind man. I was engaged in the cabin and about the decks doing duty as a cabin boy.

Everything went on right that voyage, and my ardour was not in the least abated to be a sailor. I went several voyages in the same vessel, and when I was 16 years old, I was bound apprentice to the company, for four years. I served part of my time in the Royal Sailor, and part in another of the company's vessels, called the *Duchess of Kent*, a schooner. Nothing particular happened while I was serving my time. We were once driven in bad weather to leeward of our port, and went into the Firth of Forth for shelter.

After I finished my apprenticeship I joined my old skipper, Mr. Harper, and went four voyages with him. But I became restless again, and began to wish

I was in a larger ship, and that I could go a long voyage. I made known my wish and my determination to get a larger ship, and Mr. Henry May, who was agent to the company gave me a present for good conduct, my discharge, and three letters of recommendation – one to the Sailor's Home in London, and two to large shipowners. I gave a man 5 shillings to show me the way to the Sailor's Home, where I saw several notices on the notice-board, among others a carpenter's mate was wanted for the *Ramalees*. I said carelessly that I would take it – having no intention of doing so – and some time afterwards went to bed. In the morning I heard someone asking for the man who was going as carpenter's mate on the beforementioned ship. I said I did not mean it, that I had letters to certain gentlemen which I had not yet delivered, and they would get me a ship; but I was induced to give up my shipping ticket and consent to go. So without presenting my letters, I returned home to make up my outfit of clothing and tools. Everybody was very angry with me at home for acting so hastily, and told me it was a troop ship, and that I should be anything but comfortable in her. However having given up my shipping ticket there was no alternative, for the maritime laws affecting seamen were very severe.

Barron Falls in the early part of the Dry Season (May to October).

All being ready, I left home and joined the ship at Deptford on a Friday. The following day we dropped down the stream and anchored at Gravesend. The next day, Sunday, we shipped the 11th regiment of foot for Hobart Town, whither we were bound; and a detachment of the royal artillery, for Sydney, which was intended for New Zealand – the war having broken out in the Bay of Islands. We started on our voyage some time during the week, which we were six months in accomplishing.

All troop ships were forced to carry a double complement of hands, so when we arrived at Sydney one half of us were not wanted, I obtained permission to leave the ship, for I had not been long enough from home yet, and I was anxious to see and gain as much experience as possible. I then shipped on board a little schooner lying in the cove, called the *Terror*, bound for

Auckland, New Zealand; I made a successful voyage in her to Auckland and back – we brought copper ore back with us – but not being an easy job to get a cargo in those days, some of us were discharged – myself among the number.

There were several vessels in the harbour laid on for home, but I thought I would not return yet, so I shipped on board the ill-fated ship, *Peruvian*, bound to China, with a cargo of hardwood, with what result my readers will see.

Two blacks with their weapons; a large sword-club (which Mjoberg called a "battle axe"), two painted shields, and a boomerang. They wear painted body decoration, necklaces, and waist bands. The man on the left wears a traditional pubic decoration made from human hair string or animal fur string. The man on the right wears a European leather belt (replacing the traditional waist band) and pubic decoration. Cardwell. North Queensland. (Atkinson collection, c. 1890s.)

CHAPTER 2

VOYAGE FROM SYDNEY TO CHINA – SHIPWRECK
– 42 DAYS ON THE RAFT – REACHING THE LAND
– KIND RECEPTION BY THE NATIVES – DEATH OF
MR. WILMOTT AND A SEAMAN – LIFE AMONG THE
NATIVES – DEATH OF THE APPRENTICE BOY, THE
CAPTAIN, AND HIS WIFE – RESTORATION
TO CIVILIZED LIFE.

Some 65 years after Morrill's shipwrecking, a cyclone kills 36 people and damages Mjoberg's boat off the Queensland coast. Steel as thick as a thumb is twisted and bent. The motor boat at the right is smashed, lying on its side.

On Tuesday, the 24th February, 1846, I shipped on board the ill-fated ship *Peruvian*, Captain George Pitkethley, with a full complement of hands, and passengers, as follows: – Passengers – Mrs. Pitkethley, Mr. and Mrs. Wilmott, Miss Wilmott (an infant), and a young nursegirl; Mr. J. B. Quarry, and daughter, about six years old. Ship's company – The captain, the captain's brother (first mate), John – (second mate), the carpenter, John Millar (sail maker), the cook, James Dicks, James Gooley, Jack – , and myself (able seamen); James Wilson, William – , James – , and another (apprentices); and two black men; the captain, officers, and apprentices were all of Dundee. I give the names as far as possible from memory, as there are no records in the Sydney Custom House of any but the passengers, and they are two short – the child of Mrs. Wilmott and nursegirl.

On Wednesday we finished loading, and dropped down the stream. On Thursday she was cleared at the customs, and on the sailor's unlucky day (Friday), the mail came on board, with the pilot, and we started on our voyage, with a fresh leading wind, which lasted during that day and the next. On Sunday, stunsails, main-skysails and every stitch of canvas was set, till sundown, when the weather came on threatening. All the small sails were taken in and stowed, and the wind increased very much during the night. At eight bells on the Monday morning all hands were ordered on deck to shorten sail. We got her all snug. On the following day her fine weather sails all blew away, when we got new ones bent on. The bad weather increased till Friday, when every stitch of canvas had to be taken off, and she drove under bare holes. The next day, Saturday, the weather showed signs of breaking, and the captain got sights, but it was very thick. When it moderated we got a little sail on her, to keep her steady; and at night, during the first watch, the mate made more

The middle deck on Mjoberg's boat is destroyed by a storm.

sail. The captain said that we were in the neighbourhood of Horse Shoe Reef, or the Minerva Shoal, and told us to keep a good look out for broken water. The first watch was relieved at 12 o'clock; I was in the second watch, under the charge of the second mate. I took the wheel from 12.00 to 2.00, when I was relieved by the eldest apprentice. Between the hours of 3 and 4 o'clock, we observed what appeared to be land, or a dark cloud dead ahead of us. The second mate went down and told the captain, and immediately returned on deck; he had hardly done so, however, when the ship struck with great force on a rock, and the first sea that struck her lifted her partly on the rock, and swept one of the boats and the second mate overboard, who was never afterwards seen. The next sea that struck her lifted her wholly on the top of the rocks, where she stuck fast; the first shock knocked her bilge off, and so much damaged her, that if she had been in deep water, she must have sunk quickly. The captain and all hands ran on deck in great confusion, most of whom were in their night-clothes, and finding that she was hard and fast on the rock, the sea still running very high, and not knowing where or how we were situated, we took shelter under the lea of the cuddy, till such time as we could see what was best to be done.

At daylight a terrible scene presented itself, as far as the eye could reach there were the points of the rocks awash, but no friendly land in view. The captain ordered the jolly boat to be got over the side, as that seemed our only chance of escape. We hung her in the tackles, but no sooner lowered her within reach of the water than she stove to pieces in the broken water, and became useless. We now had only the long boat left, which was old and shaky. The captain ordered us to launch it over the side, which we did, intending to keep her there till we got the passengers and provisions into her, and then cut ourselves away. But no sooner was she put over the side than the spray and broken water filled her as she hung in the tackle. The captain ordered some hands into her to bail her out, but it was so unsafe that none would risk their lives in her excepting the first mate, who was the captain's brother. Before he had got out a couple of buckets, the stern post was jirked out of her and left hanging in the tackles; at the same time the fore tackle got adrift, and she was carried away from the wreck with the force of the current. Lines were thrown out, but none reached him. There was a live sheep in the boat beside the mate. He then calmly sat in the bows of the boat, and bid goodbye to his brother and sister, awaiting the will of God; presently he disappeared from sight, and was seen no more. He could not have lived long. Our position being now apparently hopeless, the captain called us all into the cabin, where we engaged in religious exercises, and commended ourselves to God in prayer. We then went on deck again and discussed the propriety of making a raft; our chances of being picked up were so small, and not knowing but that we might be washed off our present resting place with the next sea, decided us in taking active steps in whatever we did. We accordingly set to work and cut away the spars of the ship, and fixed them – first the mizen mast, then the main mast – but it was very difficult to make use of them, for they came down with the sails all flying, and they were very much entangled. With these and some small spars we had in-board, we had enough for our purpose. The large outside spars we rested partly on the rocks and partly on the wreck; we lashed and nailed them strongly together, and in the centre we fixed a mast and platform of light spars, to enable us to sit and lay out of the water. When finished, the next difficulty was to get it adrift. With great labour we managed to get it first off the ship's quarter on to the rock all safe, and then into the water, this we accomplished by middle day Sunday. We then began to look up the provisions, and to our dismay we found the bread all utterly spoilt with salt water, and the preserved meat, which we had previously piled on deck to put in the boats was nearly all washed overboard. To add to our misfortune, there was nothing left whole that would hold water, excepting a small keg. All we could muster then was, a few tins of preserved meat, the small keg of water, and a little brandy. This being carried safely on the raft, and placed under the captain's charge, the ladies and children were got on, also the captain's instruments and charts, and some blankets and clothing. We were at last all on the raft, and it was our intention to stay by the wreck a few days, and if possible build a boat, as there were some boat planks aboard. During the night, however, the strength of the current and the dead weight of the raft, caused it to part its moorings, and we were carried to sea. There were on the raft three ladies, two children, two gentlemen passengers, the captain, carpenter, sailmaker, cook, four able seamen, including myself, four apprentices, and two black men, stowaways, working their passage – in all 21 souls.

The ship's captain, engineer and second pilot beside the starboard lifeboat damaged with a split at the back.

It was agreed that the stores should be given out equally amongst us, and that there should be no lots drawn to take away each other's lives. One table-spoonful of preserved meat a day was served out, and the water was measured in the neck of a glass bottle, four to each person – the meat about 12 o'clock in the day; the water in the morning, middle of the day, and in the evening. All went on as well as could be expected under the circumstances, for 23 days. The current and our small sail carried us about 40 miles a day; at first we caught a few birds which were a great treat, their blood was greedily drunk, and their raw flesh eaten with gusto; but as we neared the land we caught none. The weather was fine throughout; in the daytime there would be a light wind, which died away at sundown. The captain took sights occasionally. On the 22nd day out we saw a sail in the distance, which kept in sight about four hours, but finally disappeared, we having no means of attracting its attention, which greatly disappointed us.

A few days after this the first man died (James Quarry), leaving his child to survive him for a short time; he said the day before that he was dying, and that he should not live long. As soon as he died he was stripped and thrown over, the sharks devouring him instantly before our eyes. The next day we caught a fine rock cod fish with a line and hook baited with a bit of white rag, which was cut up in equal parts and served out. It then rained, but the sail was so soaked with salt water that we could not drink what we caught till the salt was well nigh washed out of it. We managed to get enough to eke out our small store before it cleared up again. The sucking child of Mrs. Wilmott was the next to die, and shortly afterwards the other little girl, and next to her Mrs. Wilmott herself died. Her husband then took off what clothing she had on, which was only a nightdress, and threw her into the sea; she remained in company with us longer than the others floating on the water, she was observed near us about 20 minutes. The burial service was read over each. At this time, they dropped off one after the other very rapidly, but I was so exhausted myself that I forget the order of their names.

We next began to think how we should obtain food, our only fishing line had been broken and carried away. We had more hooks but no more line. There were plenty of sharks about and we tried to catch them. The captain devised a plan to snare them with a running bowling knot, which we did as follows: – We cut off the leg of one of the men that died and lashed it at the end of the oar for a bait, and on the end of the other oar we put the snare, so that the fish must come through the snare to get at the bait. Presently one came, which we captured and killed with the carpenter's axe, by cutting its head off. The sailmaker was looking at its head and eating it, he put his hand in its mouth, which gave him a severe bite; he did not want any of that shark to eat, for he had quite enough by sucking his own blood. The rest of us made a fine meal off him. Three days after that we caught another one in the same way, and with the same bait, which we cut up in strips and dried. We then caught another and did the same with it. Our numbers by this time were very much reduced. Shortly after this we made the Barrier Reef; we came down upon it driven by a strong current: we managed after a great deal of trouble to get the raft clear over it into deep water before dark. Two days after this we came in sight of the land, which appears to have been Cape Upstart. We were not a long way out at sea, and at night we passed it. Two or three days afterwards we saw the land once more, and were driven towards Cleveland Bay, but just as we were preparing to get ashore in the hopes of getting water, a land breeze sprung up and drove us out to sea again. During the night, however, the sea breeze drove us in shore once more, and eventually, about midnight, we landed on the Southern Point of Cape Cleveland. One or two tried to get water but were not successful, so we laid down on the sand and went to sleep. Presently it came on to rain, which filled the holes in the rocks and from these we filled our tins. While on the raft the captain cut a notch in a piece of wood every day, and on counting them there were 42; and of the 21 who left the wreck alive only seven remained – the captain, his wife, Mr. George Wilmott, myself, James Gooley, the sailmaker, and one of the boys.

In the morning when the sun arose, we washed a dry piece of white rag; we then took a magnifying glass out of the spy-glass, set light to the rag, and made a fire. We then took some of the dried shark we had left, boiled it in a preserved meat tin, and ate it, with a drink of clear fresh water for breakfast, which we enjoyed much.

Two Aboriginal men in dense rainforest vegetation, at the edge of the north Queensland jungle. (Atkinson collection, c. 1890s.)

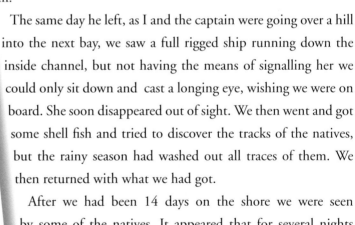

At low water, the captain, being the strongest, sallied forth in quest of food; he shortly afterwards returned for the axe, bringing a few rock oysters, which were very plentiful, sticking in large clusters to the rocks. Some of us managed to crawl and get a few and return to our camping ground, but being so long on the raft without exercise, it was very difficult to move about at first. We continued to do this for a few days, but Mr. Wilmott and the able seaman James Gooley were so exhausted, they laid down by a water hole and died, nobody being equal to provide for more than themselves. The captain found in his rambles a native canoe and lines and spears of a fishing party of natives, who had evidently been there lately in the rainy season. The sailmaker, Jack Millar, hearing of this, determined he would go away in the canoe, which he accordingly did the next morning, but we eventually knew he was starved to death on the shores of the next bay, for the natives found his body and told us of him.

Part of an ancient forest and small creek from the Atherton-Herberton highlands.

The same day he left, as I and the captain were going over a hill into the next bay, we saw a full rigged ship running down the inside channel, but not having the means of signalling her we could only sit down and cast a longing eye, wishing we were on board. She soon disappeared out of sight. We then went and got some shell fish and tried to discover the tracks of the natives, but the rainy season had washed out all traces of them. We then returned with what we had got.

After we had been 14 days on the shore we were seen by some of the natives. It appeared that for several nights they had observed falling stars in one particular direction – the direction of the rocks on which we were. They also, it afterwards appeared, have a kind of superstition in reference to falling stars; they think that they point out the direction of an hostile tribe. Something however more than usual possessed the minds of these black fellows, and they bent their steps in the direction the stars fell, and came on to the

a. b. c. d. e. f.

The types of wooden artefacts used by Aborigines varied throughout Australia, and shown here are those for the region of coastal and northern Queensland.

Four pronged wooden spear used to catch eels. Tully River, north Queensland.

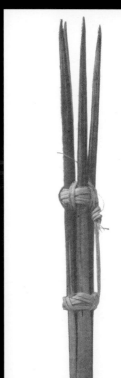

Details of six spears from north Queensland.
(a) Mjoberg was told this barb was made from a human shin bone, and it appears similar to those made from a stingray barb.
(b) Spear tip made from part of a fish or *silurid*.
(c) *Acacia* wood spear.
(d) Spear with barbs made from echidna quills.
(e) Black palm spear.
(f) Four pronged spear used to catch fish.

(a) Fish club from Cedar Creek.

(b) Spearthrower with shell handle.

(c) Spearthrower with decorated shaft.

(d) Music stick.

a.

b.

c.

d.

Men and boys from Russell River, northern Queensland, decorated with vertical lines of parrot feather down. The younger boys have more extensive feather decoration on their upper bodies and heads. Two women kneel, undecorated, at the front of the group. Various designs are painted on the large rainforest shields. These shields, along with the large sword-clubs, are used in ritualised fighting and ceremonies. (Atkinson collection, c. 1890s.)

same man as on pages 24 and
31, demonstrating hunting and
spear throwing. The spear, about
to be raised and thrown, is held
in the left hand, while the right
hand holds the spearthrower,
positioned so as to hook into
the end of the spear. When
raised to the horizontal, the
spearthrower will be used like a
lever or extended arm to propel
the spear forwards at a rate
much faster than can be achieved
otherwise.
(From motion-picture film.)

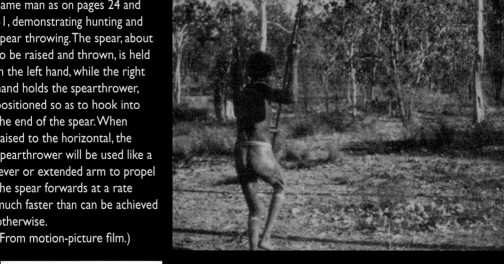

A throwing club, "*nulla nulla*",
from Cedar Creek.

A beautifully painted shield, greater than
one metre long, from Harveys Creek, north
Queensland. At the top left is beeswax which
has been used to fill in and repair gashes in the
wood from battle scars. The art on these shields
represents totemic and clan designs.

coast, where they immediately discovered fresh made tracks, which they followed up till they came to a camp fire at the place where the boy had camped the preceding night. Indeed he had only just left. He had two large boils on his leg, and was not able to get to the general camping ground the previous night, but as soon as possible in the morning he came away; and it was a few minutes after he had gone, that the blacks came on his track. They followed him up at a distance and saw him, but as there were so many tracks they did not come near nor show themselves: they tracked him down till they came to the captain's wife – I

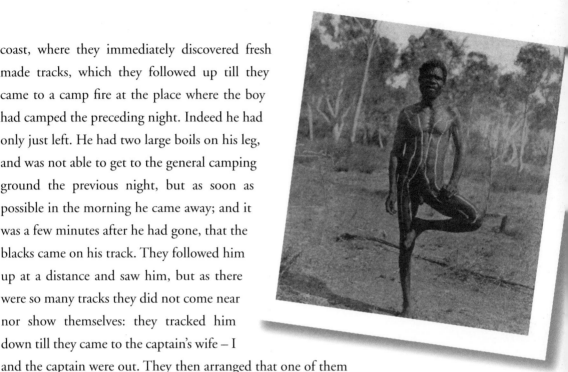

Black man resting a few minutes after a long day's journey. Typical Aboriginal resting position while standing. Coleman River, north Queensland.

and the captain were out. They then arranged that one of them should stay in sight and the other two should go to the camp and bring more of the tribe – they brought about 20 or 30. When I returned in the evening, the captain's wife said she had heard the natives jabbering and whistling; I did not think she had. When the captain came home she told him, and while we were talking about it – about 10 minutes after the captain came home – she heard the same noises again. She immediately jumped up and went outside to see what it was, she looked up on the rocks, and there, sure enough, she saw a number of the naked black fellows. She exclaimed – "Oh George, we have come to our last now, here are such a lot of the wild blacks." We went out to see, and there they were. They were as afraid of us as we were of them. Presently we held up our hands in supplication to them to help us, some of them returned it; after a while they came among us and felt us all over from head to foot. They satisfied themselves that we were human beings, and hearing us talk, they asked us by signs where we had come from. We made signs and told them we had come across the sea, and seeing how thin and emaciated we were, they took pity on us, and asked us as well as we could understand where we were going to sleep. We showed them in the rock. They came in with us, and we were going to give them some of our things, but we found while we were engaged talking, some of the others had been in and cased us of everything. Eventually about 10 of the old men came in the cave-like hollow rock that we had made our camping place, to sleep with us, and they kept us separated by laying between us. They kept up a constant jabber among themselves, which led to a second and more minute examination of our persons to ascertain our sex which seemed necessary to them on account of our being clothed. And when they found we were like themselves – male and female – they were satisfied, and did not further interfere with us. They

Elderly couple. Cedar Creek, north Queensland.

seemed to understand that the captain and his wife bore that relationship by their being always so close together, and they never afterwards troubled us. We got some light sleep during the night. At daylight the next morning, there was a great commotion among the blacks, as to what should be done with us. There were present representatives of two different tribes – the boy and myself were claimed by a tribe who had camped about Mount Elliott: and the captain and his wife were claimed by a tribe belonging to Cape Cleveland. Not content with taking all we brought with us, they commenced to strip us. They took the boy's trousers off, but he begged to be allowed to keep his shirt and sou'wester, pointing to the sun, to make them understand that it would kill him; they seemed to understand, and allowed him to retain them. They then took all the captain's clothes off; and when they came to me and the captain's wife, we made signs to them that we were afraid of the sun, so they let us retain them. Presently seeing that we had all our clothes on and that the captain was without any, they gave him his back again. They then gave us some small roots to eat, about the size of small marbles, which we ate, and enjoyed them much – they tasted like nuts. They pointed to our

Northern Queensland has varied landscapes, with open woodlands and paper bark (*Melaleuca* species) swamps over the inland, thicker forests along coastal mountain ranges, dense tropical rainforest (jungles) to the north, and beautiful coastal rivers.

OPEN WOODLAND

Aboriginal boy with his long hunting spear, standing amongst Grass Trees (*Xanthorrhoea* species) in a typical Cape York Peninsula, open forest landscape. (Atkinson collection, c. 1890s.)

Landscape with two *Eucalypt* trees in the foreground.

Large termite mounds are a typical feature of northern Australia's open woodlands.

PAPERBARK SWAMPS

Paperbark swamp (*Melaleuca* species) and water lilies, Cape York Peninsula. The paper bark is collected for wrapping things and to make homes. Its greasy nature repels water, making it an ideal shelter cover. Small pieces can also be pleated and used to carry water. The water lilies are edible food. Paperbark swamps are common in all wet areas across northern Australia.

RAINFOREST JUNGLE

Three Aborigines at the base of large Tree Ferns.
Bellenden Ker, south of Cairns. (Atkinson collection, c. 1890s.)

The Stinging Tree (*Dendrocnide moroides*, a member of the *Urticaceae* family of stinging nettles, previously described by Mjoberg, and also know as *Laportea* sp.) grows in the more open parts of north Queensland rainforests. It is covered in thick hairs that penetrate the skin and release a painful toxin if touched. However, green possums (page 36) eat the leaves.
(Atkinson collection, c. 1890s.)

Young Stinging Tree.

THICK FORESTS

Group of men, some smoking European clay pipes. They are outside one of their homes. Cedar Creek, south of Cooktown. (Atkinson collection, c. 1890s.)

Typical Queensland landscape.

COASTAL RIVERS

Landscape from the foot of Bellenden Ker, south of Cairns. Many trees had been felled by the time this photo was taken, about 1912.

stomachs, to make us understand they knew we were hungry; and to their own that they had plenty. They also pointed to the bush to tell us if we came with them, they would give us plenty to eat and drink. On our signifying our intention to go with them, they were very glad, and wanted us to join with them in a corroboree, but as we could not, we thought we should please them by singing a hymn.

I accordingly gave out a hymn I knew –

God moves in a mysterious way,
His wonders to perform, etc.

to the end, which we sung, and which amazed them much. While we were by ourselves in the cave every night, we read the bible, sung hymns, and prayed, as we had done on the raft – we had among the few books we took with us from the wreck, a prayer book, bible, and hymn book.

Next they began to make preparations to move off towards the camp – they were delighted at our going with them. Seeing the boy was unable to walk, one of them picked him up and put him on his shoulders, with his legs hanging down – the same way they carry their children when on a journey. And seeing us so weak and exhausted, two of them helped each of us along. After we had got a little way, three new arrivals came from the camp; they were told to stay somewhat in advance of us, and wait till we came up – it was on the edge of a plain – where they had made a small fire. When we came up with them they were sitting round the fire; they were powerful men, and seemed to be sitting in state, as they did not move when we came up. Great fear seized hold of me, for I thought they were chiefs; and when they came to lead me up to them to satisfy their curiosity, thinking I was going to be led up to slaughter – to be cooked and eaten – I refused and struggled against it. The fire being so small and not observing any weapons with them, it struck me they could not mean that, so I suffered myself to be led up to them, and I sat down. They looked at me and observed me shake with fear, they warmed their hands at the fire, and put them on my face, and all over my body, to reassure me, seeing which I took heart again. The captain, his wife, and the boy, underwent the same scrutiny. Here we halted for a while, and they wanted us to join them in a corroboree again, but we could not, so they had to have it among themselves. Some of them dressed themselves after a fashion with the clothes – shirts, trousers, coats, etc., that we had saved from the wreck, and a more ludicrous scene could not be imagined; one with only a sleeve of a shirt on, another with a pair of trousers on, his legs put through the bottoms, and another hind part before – some one way and some another. They also tore the leaves out of the books, and fastened them to their hair and bodies; altogether they presented a most ludicrous appearance. In the meanwhile some were sent on ahead to the camp, to tell them to make haste and get plenty to eat, and to prepare for a grand corroboree. From where we were on the sea shore to their camp was from five to eight miles, but it was sundown before we reached the camp. The first thing they did was to lay us down and cover us over with dried grass, to prevent our being seen till the appointed time. They then collected together to the number of about 50 or 60 – men, women, and children – and sat down in a circle; then those who discovered us went into the middle, dressed up in the things they had taken from us, with a little extra paint, and danced a corroboree, in which they explained in their rude song, what they had discovered, from whence they had brought us, and all they knew about us, which greatly surprised them. That being over, we were led into the middle of the ring in triumph. The sight of us – being white people, and dressed – produced a panic, and they scampered off in all directions. After a little time, however, being reassured, they returned one by one, and looked at us, and a few of the more courageous touched us; by and by they came nearer and examined us more minutely, till all fear was removed. After their curiosity had somewhat subsided, they led us to a gunyah, which was placed at our service, and they brought us plenty to eat and drink, and frequently came to make enquiries whether we wanted anything, and to have a peep at us. They went on preparing their evening meal, but one after the other they gradually

Everyday body adornments were mainly limited to waist belts and arm bands, used to carry items such as a stone knife, hatchet, or other small items. Similarly, any small lizard caught during the day could be tucked into the waist belt, leaving the hands free. More decorative items, such as necklaces and headdresses, were usually saved for wearing at ceremonial times.

A man from Atherton wearing a parrot feather headdress, a mussel shell headband, a nose bone, a necklace with a pearlshell pendant amulet, and horizontal scars over his chest and upper abdomen. The photographer has added a leaf to a modern leather belt for modesty, for a European audience. (Atkinson collection, c. 1890s.)

Two carved pearlshell
pendants in centre, the
right one with resin at one
end. Below is a mussel shell
ornament woven on string,
used as a headband.
Coleman River.

Emu feathers tied to a bone point, used to wear
as a decoration fastened into the hair.

Man holding a spear and spearthrower with shell handle. He wears an armband and waist belt made from plant fibres. This waist belt can be used to carry small items tucked around it. Cape York Peninsula.

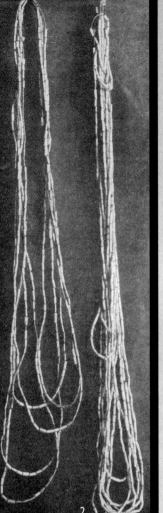

1. Necklace made from cut pieces of cane grass.
2. Necklace made from Tusk shells (*Dentalium*)
3. Hair decoration made from human hair string with native bees wax resin and three teeth from a tree kangaroo.

2.

3.

4. Covering worn over the genitals, more for decoration than to cover nudity.

4.

disappeared, and went to bed. In the morning they replenished our stock of roots and got us water, and then turned out in quest of their day's wants. As they returned they brought numbers of their relations and friends from the near tribes, and in the evening they had another corroboree, explaining all about us. When they had done, they came and fetched us into their midst, as on the previous evening, to show us to them. This was continued evening after evening for about six or eight evenings successively, as representatives from the more distant tribes came in to see the wonderful people, till the most distant known to them had seen us. This was carried on to such a length that we became worn out, and we expressed our disinclination to go; but they made us understand that they would kill us if we did not; and we thought it prudent not to put them to the test, although we believed they did not mean to do so – only to frighten us. After this, things assumed their usual course at the camp. They would not, however, let us go out to get food while we were so weak, but gathered us sufficient for all our wants. Eventually we went with them, but they dug the roots up for us till we learned to do it ourselves.

After we had been with them about five or six months, and we began to pick up their language, they made us understand that a large tribe, and a great many other tribes were coming to see us, and that they would be there in the dry season, in about four moons' time. We spent our time in wandering about with them on their fishing excursions, and in learning to snare ducks, wild turkeys, geese, and other wild fowls, which I became very expert in after awhile, much more so than the natives themselves, because I took more care in making strong string for the nooses, and in choosing the best places to set them, which made them very much attached to me.

Time ran on and the natives began to collect in large numbers – we knew them to be strange. These were the tribes we had been led to expect were coming to see us. When they all arrived, they numbered considerably over

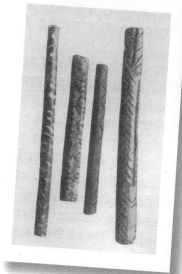

Message sticks from north Queensland. These were used like a passport, allowing a man to travel through neighbouring territory without being harmed, and to announce the invitation to a gathering of the tribes.

ABORIGINAL BUSH FOODS – INSECT, ANIMAL AND PLANT FOODS

A wide range of plants and animals were eaten, and insect foods included certain ants, grubs and beetles while streams provided fish and eels. Many birds were eaten, including waterfowl, scrub fowl, the Cassowary and the Jabiru. The yellow fat of the goanna lizard was considered a delicacy.

"Queen Adjal" and other women and children setting out for a day's walk, food collecting.
(From motion-picture film.)

he Ornate Burrowing Frog (*Limnodynastes* *natus*) from the rainforest is eaten with easure by the blacks.

Seeds from *Cryptocarya bancrofti* have to be soaked and treated before eating in order to remove their poison.

 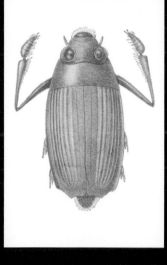 

Bibaj, an insect larva (grub) eaten by the blacks in the north Queensland rainforest. Larvae such as these are found by looking for the tell-tale signs of powder at the tree or holes in the bark, and then finding the larvae under the bark. Grubs can be eaten raw or roasted.

Whirligig Beetle (*Macrogyrus viridisulcatus*). Evelyne, north Queensland. These swim in circles on water surfaces and have split eyes allowing both underwater and above-water vision. They are collected and eaten by the Aborigines.

Wood cockroach (*Panesthia*), called *kalabaj* by the blacks, who eat it by gently crushing the shell in their teeth and then sucking out its insides.

Grey Kangaroo with its young, Cape York.

The Common Brushtail Possum (*Trichosurus vulpecula*), seen here in open savanna near the Coleman River, Cape York Peninsula, was a food source for Aborigines.

The Green Ringtail Possum (*Pseudochirops archeri*), shown here injured by a shotgun wound, is found between Townsville and the Daintree. Other species of ringtail possums are found in north and east coastal regions of Australia.

Morrill probably never saw Bennett's Tree-Kangaroo (*Dendrolagus bennettianus*) which is found around the Daintree River region, 400 kilometres north of Mount Elliott where he spent most of his time. This specimen was photographed in the Melbourne Zoo.

Two women and a child pouring *karol* (*Dioscorea sativa v. rotunda*) from a palm leaf container into a depression in the ground. Cape York Peninsula. From motion-picture film. This is a staple food, a ground vegetable (the round yam, similar to a bush potato) which needs crushing and washing to leach away its poison before it can be eaten. The plant is a root dug from under the ground, and then mashed in water. From there it is poured into a ground depression, and allowed to dry. The resulting material, similar to mashed potatoes, provides an important daily food.

Bandicoots (*Perameles*) are small Australian marsupials and different species are found throughout the country. This specimen was photographed at the Australian Museum.

A mother and her four children, Cape York Peninsula. From left to right, the baby she holds has a Chinese father, the next child has a black man as her father, this child has a white father, this child has the same black father as the older child.

a thousand souls, this was a larger number than I had ever seen before. They belonged to about l0 different tribes. We learned that some of the tribes belonged to the country far south of where we were, which determined us, if possible, to go away with them, when they returned, hoping by that means we should be able to reach some white settlement. They had a grand corroboree, which lasted about three days, and they went through the rites and ceremonies of the Boree, or making young lads men, and instructing them in their duties towards the women – hereafter described. The tribe I was in, went through their ceremonies by themselves, when about 50 lads were made men; and another tribe by themselves made only about 20. After it was all over, they began to move off to their various districts. We stole away, and went with the tribe that was going south. We were then well known to all the tribes, and we got distributed one in one tribe and one in another. The boy went down farther south than myself. The tribe I was in were located on the present site of Port Denison. Nearly two years after we had been living with them, intelligence was brought us that the boy was dead, and that they had burnt his remains, as they do the remains of their own dead. About six weeks after the boy died, the captain sickened and died also, I believe the death of the boy preyed upon his mind, and also the wretched state of his wife. Up to this time she managed by dint of great difficulty to keep herself partially covered, but he knew it could not last much longer, and the thoughts of her having to come so low, and our utter helpless condition, was too much for him – he sunk under it. The sight was too much for me, it almost broke my heart. I was forced to leave and go on a hunting and fishing expedition. I saw he could not last long, and I told them not to

Spearing fish, Babinda Creek. A man with his two sons are in the water. Two women sit on rocks on the far bank. (Atkinson collection, c. 1890s.)

1. Eel trap, made from split lengths of vine (cane). Meat is placed into the closed end as a bait, and the eels get caught inside, unable to swim backwards, and held also by the flow of the stream. Cedar Creek, north Queensland.

2. Fishing net made from fibre string fixed between two pieces of vine, which opens out like a scoop. Tully River.

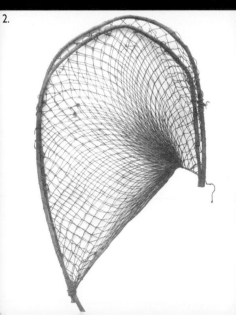

Two blacks on their outrigger canoe, fishing. Cairns. (Atkinson collection, c. 1890s.)

Outrigger canoe on the Barron River, near Cairns.

burn him, but to bury him in the ground, which they did. As soon as I heard of his death I hurried back, but before I reached the camp his wife had followed him – four days afterwards. Being in a strange tribe, I felt lonely, and I determined to go back to the tribe that claimed me as their own, thinking they would take more care of me. After several months I reached it, and they were all very glad to see me, and asked me about the others; when I told them they

were dead, they were very angry with me, and laid all the blame on me, and said I deserved a crack on the head. The tribe that the captain belonged to would have killed me if they dared, but my tribe protected me. It was the cause of a good deal of trouble between the two tribes. I was the first to go away with the captain, and when we got about 40 miles, the captain went back alone and fetched his wife and the boy, and as I did not appear, they said that it was me who had taken or decoyed them away.

After the misunderstanding was settled, I lived with the tribe year after year, as one of themselves – nothing particular happening. On one occasion when I was on the coast fishing, I saw a barque going to the north in the inner channel, but she was too far out for me to attract her attention. Shortly after this, while I was on Mount Elliott, looking for honey and bread fruit, which was not quite ripe, a report was brought to me that a vessel was seen on the coast at Cape Cleveland, where our raft had landed, and the people on board had given some of the natives some speckled shirts, which they showed me. This appears to have been Captain Till, who was on a surveying expedition.

Some time after this another vessel was seen, which was duly reported to me, and the men from the vessel went on the rocks and looked through a glass and brought down the sun to the water. I told them before, if they ever saw white men again to try and make them understand that there was a white man living there with them; they tried their utmost to do this, but seem to have failed; the white men became alarmed, and thought they meant mischief, whereas it was only their earnestness in trying to make them understand. The following quotations from the report of the proceedings of the Government schooner, *Spitfire*, in 1860, will explain this report.

"Saturday, 15th September. Having been hove to during part of the night, we bore up at daylight, with Cape Cleveland bearing W. ½ S. about nine miles distant, and at 9.30 a.m. came to in its roadstead. Fixing on a convenient rocky promontory for making observations for latitude and longitude, we landed, and perceiving a small party of natives, I was in hopes that such friendly intercourse would take place as would enable us to gather information respecting the mouth of the Burdekin. Such hopes, however, were soon blighted; for upon an increase of their party, they suddenly made an attack, which was instantly repulsed; when they retreated with great rapidity.

"Observing a canoe passing round one of the points into a lagoon, we gave chase; and after it was deserted, we took possession, and broke it to pieces so as to cut off the communication, and prevent any immediate increase to the force of the aborigines, already numerous and violently hostile.

"Sunday, 16th September. During this day we observed considerable numbers of natives about the beaches and hills, shrieking and yelling most diabolically; finally towards the evening (as we did not land on this day), they retired towards the south."

Nothing is said in the report about shooting the natives, but one stout able-bodied black fellow, a friend of mine, was shot dead by someone in the boat, and another was wounded; and the hideous yelling was the noise they usually made over their dead.

About three years ago there was a report brought to me by

The spectacular Wallaman Falls are located 35 miles (52 kilometres) from the coastal town of Ingham, and 150 kilometres north west of Mount Elliott, where Morrill stayed. They are Australia's largest single drop waterfall, being 900 feet (300 metres) high.

the blacks of a distant tribe, that a white man had been seen with two horses. Some of a tribe were lamenting the death of an old man, and while doing so, this white man fired in among them, and shot the son of the old man, who was lying on his dead body. The rest ran away; but eventually they apparently made friends of each other, and they got him off the horse, but by a preconcerted signal massacred him and tried to kill the horses, thinking they could speak and do mischief as the man had done, but they got away. Mr. P. Somers, of Port Denison, told me it would most likely be a Mr. Humphrey, who had left the party he was out with, in search of runs, intending to go by a new track. After this, four stray cattle were seen in our district, but I was on the coast with one of the blacks – my brother-in-law, making a possum skin rug. When I came back they showed me the tracks of the cattle, and I recognised them as being cattle. I questioned them about them; they said three had teats, and one had none, thus I understood three were cows and one was a bull. I told them they were what we ate, and they chaffed me about their great size, long tails, big ears and horns. That made me uneasy, I began to think that civilized life was not far off, and it considerably raised my hopes of being restored to civilization. Soon afterwards, a report came into camp of a lot of white and black men on horseback, near Cape Upstart, shooting down the tribe that I had been living with, when the captain died, at Port Denison. They explained to me about the saddles for the men to sit in, the stirrups, bridles, guns, smoke, and the noise it made when fired; and asked me if it was so with us. I told them yes, and explained it all to them, which surprised them much. On hearing this, I travelled south to the Burdekin River (*Mall Mall*, native name) thinking my chances would be greater on the river than at Mount Elliott – 50 miles further inland. My tribe kept coming backwards and forwards, and they asked me why I did not come back as I had lived with them so long, they began to suspect something. I told them I would by and by, but I told them from the first that I had a wife and two children, knowing they would not think it so strange at my wanting to get away. At last I told them I wanted to see the white men, for myself – to see if they knew my people – and to get

The range of containers here include the large baskets of woven cane from the rainforests, string bags made from string twisted from plant fibres, usually the bark of certain trees, and a water container made from folded bark and sealed with native bees wax resin.

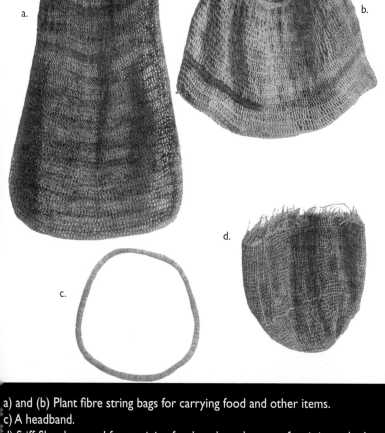

a.

b.

d.

c.

a) and (b) Plant fibre string bags for carrying food and other items.
c) A headband.
d) Stiff fibre bag used for straining food, such as the yam after it is washed

Three women from Atherton outside their hut, making baskets. Although people have few possessions, every hut has these five main items; a grindstone, a bark water container, one of these large baskets, the large battle sword-club, and a large shield. (Atkinson collection, c. 1890s.)

Bark water container, sealed with native bees wax. Malanda, south of Cairns.

Cane basket made from split Lawyer Cane / Vine (*Calamus caryotoides*). Usually called a "bicornual" basket, the correct term is "bicornuate" basket, named after its two horn-like pointed corners. Cedar Creek, north Queensland.

Some half-civilised black women from Kuranda, sitting outside their primitive hut. They are displaying beautifully woven bicornuate baskets.

Stakes stuck into the ground to hurt the feet of someone following you. They were placed on a path, next to a fallen log, so that they were not easily seen. As the person jumped down from the log, they would land on them. Evelyne, north Queensland.

clothes, and guns, and old iron, and that I would come back again. They then gave me up, and let me do as I liked, as they saw I was bent on going. From this time forward I received almost daily reports of the white people. There were two white men and a black boy constantly in the neighbourhood where I was – the black boy being a great favourite among the gins. I was about a moon-and-a-half from the place where they were, at one of our fishing grounds *(Bokodally)*, and I left to try and see them, but could not. So I returned to our head camping ground again. I shortly after heard of the cattle being on the river in great numbers, and of a man being on horseback with a stock whip which he cracked, and they thought it was a gun, on hearing which, they got up the trees quite frightened. They saw him get off the horse and drink some water with his hands, but the water being hot he scraped the sand aside and got some cool, a little black dog was with him lying on the sands. They described to me that there were so many cattle, that they had drunk all the water that was in the hole, they said they would have got the fish out only they were too much afraid. Hearing this, I was very anxious to find out the white settlement, for I felt sure there was one not very far off, but having been with the blacks so long, they were not willing to let me go, telling me I should be mistaken for a black fellow. And hearing of the blacks having guns, I could not make it out, and was afraid myself, lest if I met one of the black fellows he would not be able to understand me, and I could not tell whether I should be able to make a white man understand me, having been away so long. The next news I heard was that about 15 black fellows of a fishing party belonging to the tribe I was living with, were shot down dead. I told them it served them right: if they would let me go to them and show me where they were, I might be the means of saving their lives. They reasoned among themselves that what I said was true, and they agreed to go on a hunting expedition, on a hill called by the natives *(Yamarama)*, which was about half a mile from the station. But thinking that the white men were the same as themselves, they were not sure whether they were there. When we got to the hill, we spread our nets and commenced our work, and while we were hunting the old women went down as spies to look for the white men. They brought word back that there was a large hut, and that they had seen red and white blankets hanging on the stockyard fences, and heard a dog bark, and an old sheep bleating tied up to a tree; they also heard the report of a gun twice, but could not see where it came from. I then wanted to go and see for myself, but the man I was living with was not willing without somebody was with me. So he made his gin go with me. When we got clear of the hill going down towards the hut, we saw the sheep feeding in the grass, the sight of which so frightened the gin, she not having seen any before, that she ran back. I looked at the sheep but could not see the shepherd; so I went further on and came to a water hole, where I washed myself to make myself as white as possible. I went on still further till I came to the sheep pens, and saw the blankets and sheep as the gin had told me. I also saw the smoke of the fire in the hut, and heard noises. I stood behind the yard some minutes, not knowing what to do, and how best to make myself known. Presently I took courage and got on the fence to prevent the dogs from biting me, and called out so that they might hear me, "What cheer, shipmates." There were three staying in the hut, but there were only two at home then. They heard me, and knowing it to be a strange noise, one of them came out and saw me there – neither black nor white – naked and looked surprised; he went in again and told his mate. I understood him to say, come out Bill, here is a red or a yellow man standing on the rails, naked, he is not a black man, and bring the gun. But before they had time to use the gun, I said "do not shoot me, I am a British object – a shipwrecked sailor." Of course I meant subject, but in the excitement of the moment I did not know what I said. One said to the other "he says he is a shipwrecked sailor" – one of the men's names it appears was Hatch, the other Wilson, who had been a sailor himself – and they told me to come round the stockyard; which I did – they meeting me half way – they cross-questioned me, and I told them when and where I was wrecked, and all about my misfortunes. They asked me whether I knew what day and what date it was. I told them no, they then told me that it was Sunday, the 25th of January, 1863. They reckoned back to 1846, when I was lost, and told me it was 17 years, and asked me if I thought it was so long. I said no not half so long. After talking some time they took me in the hut and gave me a piece of bread, and asked me if I knew what it was. I told them it was made with flour, I tried to eat a piece, but I was so overjoyed that it stuck in my throat and I could not get it down. Besides, I was not hungry, for we had caught 20 small grey wallabies during the day and we had had plenty to eat. They gave me some tea, and asked me if I knew what it was, I said yes, but that it was too sweet. I had not been accustomed to sugar, and so they put some water to it. After I had been in the hut for some time they told me to look out and tell them what I saw. I saw a large flock of sheep with their third companion – coming home; he was a Scotsman, named Creek. They then wanted to give me some clothes, but I told them I had better go back to the natives who were on the hills in the distance, where we had been hunting all day, just as I was to tell them to go away towards the sea coast; and I would return in the morning, which they agreed to, and instructed me to tell them, that if they did not interfere with us, we should not interfere with them. They also told me that if I did not come back in the morning they should conclude I had told them a lie, and that they would put the black trackers on our track and shoot us.

When I left them I went back to the hills to the blacks, and they began to surround me and ask me whether I had seen the white people, and how many there were, I was obliged to tell them that there were a great many people, many more than themselves, and plenty of guns, and that if they went near they would be killed before they got there. I told them the white men had come to take their land away. They always understood that might, not right, is the law of the world, but they told me to ask the white man to let them have all the ground to the north of the Burdekin, and to let them fish in the rivers; also the low grounds, they live on to get the roots – ground which is no good to white people, near the sea coast and swampy. They asked me what I intended to do. I told them I was going to stay that night, but in the morning I must go back, or they would come and track me up and shoot us all. They said perhaps they are doing so now. I assured them they were not, but that we must go further away. So we went four or five miles and camped. The next morning they all came round me again, and finding I was bound to go, they asked me if I would be back again in a few days. I told them no, I should be away quite three or four moons. They then said you will forget us altogether, and when I was coming away the man I was living with burst out crying, so did his gin, and several of the other gins and men. It was a touching scene. The remembrance of their past kindness came full upon me and quite over-powered me. There was a short struggle between the feeling of love I had for my old friends and companions, and the desire once more to live a civilized life, which can be better imagined than described.

I left them and came on to the hut. The men were glad to see me and they took me down to the water hole, washed me with soap and flannel, and brought me up and gave me some clothes. That day we tried to cross the river to get to the head station to obtain a supply of rations, but it was too swollen. We came back, and at night they killed a sheep and cooked me a chop off it. I remained a fortnight and then gave myself up to Mr. Meyers, who left me in charge of Mr. Salting, of Hiffling cattle station until the return of the commissioner's orderly from the Fanning River, who accompanied me safely into the town of Bowen. I experienced great kindness from Mr. W. H. Thomas and Mr. P. Somers, who gave me clothes and made a subscription for me.

CHAPTER 3

THE ABORIGINALS – NOMADIC HABITS – LIVING
IN TRIBES – WHAT THEY EAT AS FOOD – LANGUAGE
– HOW THE NATIVES MAKE FIRE – THE CEREMONY
OF MAKING THE LADS MEN – RELATIONSHIP –
HOW THEY DISPOSE OF THE DEAD – FLAX GROWN
AND THE USES THEY MAKE OF IT – DESCRIPTION
OF THE COUNTRY – GOLD – EXTINCTION OF
THE RACE – APPEAL FOR THE NATIVES.

One day old. Laura,
Cape York Peninsula.

Lump of kaolin (white
clay) eaten by women
to cause abortion and
to prevent pregnancy.

The aboriginals among whom I have been living, are a fine race
of people, as to strength, size, and general appearance; but like
those of other parts of this colony, they are treacherous, jealous,
and cunning. They are not black, they are more of the colour of
half-castes. When born they are nearly white, but when they are three
days old, the gins squeeze their own milk on them, and rub charcoal
into their skins to make them black and shine. They have sunken eyes,
broad noses – which are made so by their parents in infancy
– and broad mouths. The infants are allowed to suck at
the breast a long while, indeed, until they are old enough
to get their own food. I have seen a child sucking at the
breast with its next brother or sister. I have also seen the
little things working in the swamps with their mothers,
setting roots, and every now and then go and take a suck
at the breast. The women have very few children, seldom
exceeding four, and very seldom more than one at a time.
I know of about four cases of twins. I also remember that in one case
when there was a boy and a girl born to a woman, the father killed the boy
and saved the girl – to save the trouble of bringing them up – for they are
very lazy. It caused, however, a great disturbance in the camps among their

The type of housing people used depended on the available resources for building. In woodland, large trees have relatively soft stringybark which can be chopped away in sheets and used to make simple housing. In dense rainforests, palm fronds are numerous and these are used instead.

A group of rainforest people outside one of their palm leaf huts, with the dark, ancient forest in the background. Atherton-Herberton, north Queensland (Atkinson collection, c. 1890s.)

An elderly couple commencing their hut on the edge of the ancient forest. This shows the wooden frame of interlocking sticks before the palm leaves are applied. When making these homes, the men build the wooden frame while the women collect the palm fronds. Atherton, north Queensland (Atkinson collection, c. 1890s.)

Two naked women carrying large sheets of paperbark (*Melaleuca* species) with which to make their hut. One carries her child. Cape York Peninsula, from motion-picture film. In woodland areas certain trees can provide large sheets of bark ideal for making shelters.

A small bark shelter (*gunyah*) built over a wooden frame, used in woodland areas. These men accompanied Mjoberg on his expedition.

friends, who thought they ought to have brought them up. The women go in the swamps the next day after their confinement as usual, to gather food, as though nothing had happened. The men have several wives – in some instances as many as eight or nine – and it is about their wives that all their wars, fights, and feuds occur; they steal them from each other and frequently lend them, or sell them for a time, for a slight consideration.

They never stay long in a locality, as soon as one place becomes a little exhausted of food they travel to another. In the wet and cold season they put up small gunyahs to live in, but in no particular order. They live in tribes, each tribe speaking a different dialect, it can hardly be called a different language; I could speak eight of these dialects. They have no chiefs – the strongest is the best man.

They get their living by fishing, hunting, digging in the earth for roots, gathering fruits, etc. They can eat anything; among other things sharks, alligators, shrimps, shell fish, and fish of all kinds. Kangaroos, rats, wallabies, snakes, grubs, snails, and all kinds of creeping things. Wild ducks, geese, turkeys, several kinds of roots, one of which grows at the tops of the mountains, is the best eating, called *(moogoondah)*, it is white, sweet, firm, dry, and grows in red clay soil. There is another lower down, at the foot of the mountains, in the scrub, called *(malboon)*, which is soft and more moist, and is very nice eating. There is another root rather of a sticky nature when cooked, which grows on the mountains, not in the scrub, but in the grass, and white, like a turnip, with a small thin leaf, called *(cornool)*. There is another, smaller and darker in its colour, but in other respects very much like it, called *(cahnan)*. Another, a creeper, which grows on the high banks of the freshwater rivers, with a small green leaf, the leaves very thick, called *(booan)*. There is another similar to a turnip, but smaller, called *(manoon)*. There is one which runs in and out among the grass, with a little blue flower, called *(cardoola* or *carlmbar)*, and many others more or less like them. They have several kinds of fruits, a plum, very large, but very little flesh on it, all stone nearly, called *(cowan gowan,* or *oolubba)*. There is a small currant, very blue in colour, but nearly all stone, called *(moorgah mudda)*. A wild banana, full of black seed, and very little flesh. There is also a white berry, similar to the white currant, very sweet, called *(walba)*. There is another, which is red, nearly all stone, called *(mooray)*. There is a fruit like an apple, called *(barkabah)*; a red fig, called *(cowarah)*; and a black one called *(ballamoo)*. The bread fruit grows on the mountains, called *(margurdah)*.

Father and son, showing the traditional cicatrices (scars) on their chests. Johnstone River, north Queensland.

Some coconuts used to wash ashore sometimes, I suppose from the other islands, as I never saw them growing in my rambles. There is plenty of honey in the hollows of the trees, from the native honey bees. They eat honey, combs, and bees too if they are hungry. There is plenty to eat if they are not too lazy to fetch it. Human flesh cannot be considered a part of their food, although they sometimes eat it. They eat young men killed in battle, or if killed by accident, also young women and children, but never those of their enemies. They cut their enemies up in strips, dry them, and distribute the pieces through the tribe, by which means they think they have their enemies' strength added to their own, and that they will be lucky in hunting and fishing.

They have no written language whatever, and consequently very little tradition. It is very guttural in sound, and extremely limited in power of expression. Of course they have no means of teaching their language but by imitation and memory, assisted by their wants. The different animals are arranged according to the size of their feet, hence the sheep have the same name as their wallabies *(cargoon)*; all kinds of sailing vessels have the same names as their canoes, because they float on the water *(woolgoora)*. The heavenly bodies are named differently, the sun is *(ingin)*, which they think is a body of fire, because of its warmth, and especially so since they saw us light rag with a burning glass. The moon *(wurboonburra)*, they say is a human being, like themselves, and comes down on the earth, and they sometimes meet it in some of their fishing excursions. They say one tribe throws it up and it gradually

People climbed trees to catch animals and reach native beehives for honey. Wax from the beehives was used to seal water containers (eg. page 46), and as a resin to make weapons and for decoration (eg. pages 32 and 78). In these photos, strong jungle vines are used like ropes to assist tree climbing.

1.

2.

1. A savage about to walk up a Eucalyptus tree. Cedar Creek.

2. Climbing with the use of a vine, he makes his way up the tree.

3.

3. The black is resting on the trunk of the tree. To do this, he winds the vine around his right knee to hold him up, and secures the end of the vine with his big toe.

4. Up the tree looking for wild honey.

4.

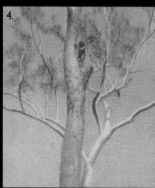

Tree climbing with a vine used as a rope. Malanda, south of Cairns.

In the rainforest, Paddy and Frank, Mjoberg's assistants, climb trees looking for possums in the tree canopy.

As agile as a monkey, a black walks up a coconut palm. Cairns.

Using a vine like a rope, the man climbs an enormous Eucalypt tree to reach animals and bush honey. Cairns. (Atkinson collection, c. 1890s.)

Black man climbing a tree, hugging it like a monkey. Cape York Peninsula. (From motion-picture film.)

He has caught a young possum, and is just about to throw it down to his friends below.

rises and then comes down again, when another tribe catches it to save it from hurting itself. They accordingly think there is a new sun and moon every day and night. There is a large open space on Mount Elliott with not a vestige of vegetation on it, whilst up to the very margin of it is a thick scrub, and they told me it was done by the moon, which once threw its circle stick round it, meaning its boomerang, and cut it off. Throwing the sun and moon up by one tribe and catching them by another, will easily be recognised as their explanation of the rising and setting of those bodies. They have no knowledge of the earth beyond the locality they inhabit. The stars and comets are both the same in name *(nilgoolerburda)*. They think the falling stars indicate the direction of danger, and that comets are the ghosts or spirits of some of their tribe, who have been killed at a distance from them, working their way back again, and that they come down from the clouds on the coast. We saw one this last dry season which they thought was one of the tribe who had been killed in war. They think all the heavenly bodies are under their control; and that when there is an eclipse, some of their tribe hide it with a sheet of bark to frighten the rest. About six years ago, there was nearly a total eclipse of the sun, the only one I saw. I asked an old man what it meant, and he told me his son had hid it *(the sun)* to frighten another of his tribe. But they are very uneasy during its continuance. They pick up a piece of grass and bite it, making a mumbling noise, keeping their eyes steadily fixed on it till it passes over, when they become easy again and can go to sleep comfortably. They think they have power over the rain *(durgun)* to make it come and go as they like. The rainbow *(terebare)* they think, is the clouds spewing fish in the lagoons, and roots on the hills, or something for their good, wherever the end points. They are very frightened at thunder *(teegoora)*, and lightning *(timulba)*, although I never knew an instance of any harm being done with the lightning. They have no knowledge of how they came into existence, they think they live and die like dogs, but there is a kind of innate fear of death, and they have some thought that they will jump up white fellows; the reference to their friends in the comets points to some undefined hereafter, but the knowledge of the future is nearly obliterated. They told me that their forefathers witnessed a great flood, and nearly all were drowned, only those who got on a very high mountain (*Bibbiringda,* which is inland of the north bay of Cape Cleveland) were saved. I understood them to refer to the flood mentioned in scripture, especially as they say only a few were allowed to go up.

They can only count five – *(Woggin)* 1, *(Boolray)* 2, *(Goodjoo)* 3, *(Munwool)* 4, *(Murgai)* 5. For any number beyond these, they put up their 10 fingers together; beyond that again, the 10 fingers of another person, and so on for three or four persons, till they come to a moon; and when they refer to fish, roots, or things in general, they can only say a few or plenty. They measure time by moons and wet and dry seasons.

The language is very irregular, and it seems to me totally impossible to systematise it in any way. The following is a list of the principal words: -

Nannie – earth	*Durgun* – rain
Ejugabah – fire	*Telebare* – rainbow
Doongalla – water	*Teegoora* – thunder
Ingin – sun	*Timulba* – lightning
Wurboonburra – moon	*Moggoor* – clouds
Nilgoolerburda – stars, comets	*Bundara* – sky

Munyah – man	*Cabankabun* – hands
Youngoorah – woman	*Coode* – head
Mowdruman – boy	*Teeburra* – eyes
Murgunman – girl	*Deeragun* – ears
Colaman – babies	*Weir* – hair
Deenah – feet	*Telli* – tongue
Tabaray – legs	*Tingool* – teeth
Toobun – arms	*Moolin* – lips

Mooda Mooda – neck
Ugar – breast
Nhamoon – teats

Booloo – belly
Doolga – back

Woolgoora – canoe, ships
Cargoon – sheep, named after
small kangaroos on the mountains.
Cockool – cattle, named after large
kangaroos.
Oombal – horses, named after
dogs.
Oodra – kangaroo, large, on the
plains (male).
Bourgoola – kangaroo, large, on
the plains (female).
Coondoola – emu
Prorogwan – native companion
Moongun – oppossum, or wild cat
Munbrebare – flying squirrel
Cundulmule – wood, or kangaroo
rat, because of hoof of the foot
being like a kangaroo's.
Kooroongun – common rat
Gungur – iguana (green, harmless),
there are three kinds of iguanas.
Coonbinmulla – light dark speckles,
short thick tail (harmless).
Coobirangil – all one colour, light
brown (rather dangerous).

Carbul – carpet snake (very
harmless and good eating).
Carmoomulle – black snake, yellow
belly, lives both in the water and
on the land.
Othubuda – a long thin light
brown snake, lives in the grass, to
be bit by which is certain death.
They have no antidote against
snake bites.
Dungaburre – a large brown snake.
Bindebudda – a large brown snake,
with red spots on its belly, these
are all good eating.
Mooraynburra – turkey, named
after the red currant, because they
are very fond of it.
Booloon – albatross
Noogooral – goose
Yamarah – duck
Waboora – small
Wadoolbil – large
Queearilla – plenty
Enugedy – enough, that will do.

The natives get fire by friction, by rubbing two soft pieces of wood of the same kind together, they generally use the wood of the black fig as being the easiest. They take a branch off, a little thicker than your finger, split it up and put it on the ground, the flat side upwards, and hold it down with their feet; they then take a sound piece, round and straight, about 12 inches long, and put one end on the flat side of the piece on the ground, holding it up between their hands, and then commence rolling it rapidly between them, pressing it into the piece beneath, so that it begins to make a hole in it, as though they were boring it; after they have done that for a minute or two, they make a notch on the side of the piece at the bottom, so that the fine dust they make while the boring process is going on shall fall down on some dry grass they have there to catch it, they then repeat the rolling process till the sparks come, at last pick up the dry grass with the dust in it, and blow it till it lights up.

The ceremony of making the lads young men, takes place about once every six years. They had four ceremonies of this kind while I was with them. For eight or nine months immediately previous, they have to go in the bush to provide for themselves, during which time they are never allowed to see a female, this is to test their fitness to take a wife; if they do see a female, they think they will waste away. After the nine months are over they are brought into the camp, cane rings are put on their arms and tightened very much, so as to stop the circulation of the blood. Their arms swell very much, which puts them in great agony. They are then left in that torture all night – their cries are terrible to hear. To keep their fingers from contracting and thus deforming them, they sit with their hands and fingers spread out on the ground, with the heels of their feet tightly pressed on them. In the morning they are brought into the presence of their mothers, sisters, and relatives; and just above and below the mark of the cane ring on their arms they make small incisions to let the blood flow and prevent inflammation. While this is being done, their mothers and relatives are crying and cutting themselves from head to foot with sharp stones, in token of joy at seeing them. When this is somewhat subsided, places are provided for them to sleep under, with boughs to shade them from

Mjoberg published this sequence of images taken from his cinematography (movie picture) film, showing a man lighting his fire from two sticks, then cooking and eating a large snake. Cape York Peninsula.

1. Making Fire. First, the vertical (upper) fire stick is twirled between the hands, boring into the lower fire stick, held against the ground by the left foot. This drilling action produces red hot powdery sawdust-ember, which is then collected and placed into a wad of fine, crushed grass (tinder). Cape York Peninsula. (From motion-picture film)

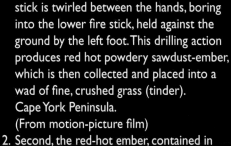

2. Second, the red-hot ember, contained in the small clump of dried grass tinder, is blown on and swung about to create wind which heats the ember so that it glows red and thus ignites the tinder. In the photo, smoke is produced just seconds before the grass bursts into flame.

3. This flame is then added to firewood and blown upon, producing fire.

4. The hungry black is roasting his meal – a really large python. He is seen placing the dead snake on the fire in order to cook and eat it.

5. He bites pieces of delicious, dripping fat from the snake's back. Note he has placed his spear upright into the ground at the right, with his spearthrower placed upright, resting against the spear.

Fire sticks. The upper stick is the one held vertically and twirled. The lower stick has a small depression at the right, with a notch off to the lower side. This stick is placed on the ground, and for a right handed operator, the left foot is placed over the left part of the stick. The top stick is twirled in this depression, producing hot ember which falls to the side, out the notch, and is collected on dry material below.

A torch made from dried palm fronds and twisted rattan (split vine). Torches are used for night fishing and hunting, and night travel. Cedar Creek, north Queensland.

the sun, as they could of course get no sleep during the night. While they are sleeping the old gins go into the swamps and get roots to make cakes for them, and the men get all the spears the young men have been carrying with them during the nine months they have been away, and fix them in the earth on a clear space in a semi-circle, fastening grass festoons from head to head of the spears. In the evening all being ready, they wake up, generally about 80 in number, and they are each seated under a festoon in a reclining position. Then their sisters or female cousins lay with their heads on their arms, to press down the swollen or cut places, and they believe nothing harmful will come of it after that. While they are laying there, a lot of cakes are thrown up and scrambled for by the lookers on, who had gone through the ceremony before them; they then go to their several fires. In the morning they are taken a little way in the bush again, and dressed up with shells, and the down of birds stuck on their heads, painted, and made to look to the best advantage, they are then brought back to choose and take their sweethearts, and the whole ceremony closes with a grand corroboree.

After this is over there is a good deal of quarrelling and fighting among them. They steal the wives of the old and weak men, and daughters from their parents, which leads to fighting, and often extends between two tribes, and then there is a war, which is not, however, of a very sanguinary nature. They often get some terrible blows, and sometimes one gets killed, but they cannot keep it on many hours, for they are forced to go and get supplies in the shape of food, in the swamps, and they seldom renew the conflict.

They are very strict in their relationship. When girls are about 10 years old they are not allowed to sleep with their brothers at the same fire. The intended mother-in-law of a young man is not allowed to look at him, until such time as the before-mentioned ceremony is over. And as families they are very distinct. They burn their dead, and for 12 months carry the burnt remains about tied up in a sheet of bark, and afterwards, throw it into a water hole. Their tomahawks *(bullgoo)* are made of stone, and latterly they have got a good deal of iron *(bingulburra)* amongst them, with which they make a kind

Four Aboriginal men painted and decorated, performing a simple dance. Cape York Peninsula (From motion-picture film.)

The dance continues at a really slow pace.

Mission blacks preparing for a dance, painted and carrying their spearthrowers. Yarrabah. (Taken from motion-picture film.)

A secret meeting, called *"yabba yabba"*, at a distant place in the forest. Here, the leader of his people, who are sworn to be faithful to him, decides the most important questions. Men and boys are ceremonially decorated with feather down attached to their skin, carrying large shields, spears, boomerangs and a sword-club. They are standing around an old tree stump. North Queensland. (Atkinson collection, c. 1890s.)

of chisel, by fastening a piece between two pieces of wood with which they make their spears, boomerangs, etc.

There is very fine flax grown there, which they find very useful in making their fishing and hunting nets. They make very good mesh nets. They place their net for hunting in the most frequented paths of the kangaroo, or whatever they are hunting for, and they then go and beat them up and drive them in. They catch a great many birds with snares, merely loose knots, which are placed in the thick grass and reeds in the swamps, and as the birds go through in quest of food, in the night, they are caught.

The country about Mount Elliott, where I have been living is well watered and grassed. It is very low and swampy in many places. There is abundance of fresh water. At the top of Mount Elliott there is a never-failing spring of beautiful water, which finds its way down exactly opposite sides of the mountain. It is such a thick scrub, and there is such an abundance of food in it, and plenty of water, that if the aboriginals were driven from the country all around they would find a safe asylum there. There are a great many alligators in both the fresh and salt water creeks, and particularly in one large freshwater lagoon. I have seen dozens of natives dragged down and killed by them. I had a scratch on my knee from one myself, the scar of which I shall carry to my grave. I was also bitten by a whip snake, which made me swell up for two days. I have seen dozens die from the bites of snakes.

I have frequently been asked if I knew whether it was a gold bearing country. Not having had any experience, even by report, of such countries, I cannot tell. I remember once when out, looking for some coloured earths to paint myself with, I picked up a piece of what I thought to be coloured ochre, but it was very heavy and hard. I also remember once when on Mount Elliott, I was getting stones for tomahawks, etc., that they were very much like those I have seen in the jeweller's shop windows in Queen Street, with pieces of yellow metal in them, but whether it was gold I know not, I should think it was not, if it had been, it would probably have occurred to me.

The work of extinction is gradually but surely going on among the aboriginals. The tribe I was living with are far less numerous now than when I went among them. What with the wars, fights, destruction by the settlers and black police, and the natural deterioration in the people themselves, they are fast disappearing. During the time I was among them, I suffered a great deal from rheumatism, which has left its mark on me, so much so, that I have very little strength left, and I feel I should not have lasted much longer amongst the natives.

Two blacks from Cape York Peninsula smoking a bamboo pipe. Native tobacco, *pituri*, was traded from the inland and normally mixed with ashes and chewed. When pipes were introduced to the Aborigines, *pituri* was smoked like tobacco.

It will perhaps be pardonable in me if I refer to a suggestion thrown out by a correspondent in the Courier newspaper, to the effect that the natives who were so kind to me should be dealt with in a similar manner, as those who succoured Burke, Wills and King. I would just call attention to what I previously mentioned; almost their last wish to me was with tears in their eyes that I would ask the white men to let them have some of their own ground to live on. They agreed to give up all on the South of the Burdekin River, but asked that they might be allowed to retain that on the other, at all events that which was no good to anybody but themselves – the low swampy grounds near the sea coast. It would be useless to send them flour, they would not eat it, not knowing anything about it; nor cattle or sheep, they would run away from them with fear, besides if they once understood the use of them as food, it would make it more dangerous to the settlers, but a good blanket would be invaluable, so would some small tomahawks, knives, old iron hoops, and fishing hooks.

POSTSCRIPT

Following his return to civilisation, **James Morrill** married and had a son. He worked with the Department of Customs in Bowen and acted as interpreter and intermediator between settlers and Aborigines, helping to prevent confrontation between the two groups. He also advised settlers on his knowledge of the country, its climate, and the people, and went on a further sea expedition along the Queensland coast, north of Bowen.

Morrill died on 30th October 1865 and is buried in the Bowen cemetery. The newspaper of the day described his death as being from rheumatism, inflammation and fever, following the effects of his knee wound. It is possible that his knee wound, the result of a crocodile bite while with the Aborigines, could have festered for some years and developed osteomyelitis (bone infection), then flared up and produced septicaemia (blood borne infection), fever, and death.

Further botanical information was given by Morrill to Monsieur Thozat who published the notes in the Rockhampton Bulletin of 14th March, 1866:

> The importance of Morrill's experience would have been practically illustrated had his services been at the disposal of the late lamented Victorian Expedition by the preservation of Burke and Wills' lives, through his knowledge of indigenous articles of food, and the consequent certainty of their ultimate return to relate their own achievements. But Fate otherwise willed it, and Providence appears now to have conferred upon us a means of averting the recurrence of similar disasters. With the above preface, then, we will at once plunge in medias res, and commence our botanical recapitulation with the native small plum, aboriginally known as the *Balemo,* botanically as the *Ficus aspera,* R. Br., a shrub occasionally verging into a small tree, and pointed out by Morrill on the northern range of the Fitzroy. This

plant can be readily identified by its oval dark green leaves, which, like its specific name, indicates its singular roughness. The milky juice of the young shoots is employed by the natives medicinally, and is represented by Morrill, from personal experience, to be very efficacious in healing wounds. After the application of the milky juice of the *Balemo*, the scraped root bark of the *Ourai*, or *Grewia* of botanists, a genus belonging to the *Tiliaceae* order, is employed as a poultice to the wound – it is to be presumed from its emollient properties, as a counterbalance to the acridity of the *Balemo*. The *Ourai* or *Grewia* grows abundantly near Rockhampton, and has a large alternate oval serrated leaf, tomentose beneath, bearing as fruit a very small brown berry generally in pairs, on a small axillary peduncle. The Rockhampton tribe call this plant *Karoom*. The two plants, the *Balemo* and the *Ourai*, are the only two Morrill could identify in the Rockhampton flora as in use by the natives both medicinally and as edibles.

The following are the other vegetable foods from which Morrill derived a considerable portion of his sustenance. The *Barkaba*, or botanically, *Barringtonia careya*, Roxd., occasionally locally denominated the broadleaved apple tree, very common in our rich alluvial soil, bearing a handsome pink and white flower; the fruit is full of seed, and tasting not unlike a dry banana. According to Morrill the bark of the stem of the *Barkaba* is used by the natives for stupefying fish in fresh water and, strange to say, the bark of the root for the same purpose in salt water. The *Kaourou*, or *Nymphaea gigantea*, Hook, the well known blue water lily, common in our lagoons, is another edible plant, its seed and root forming an important item of aboriginal diet in addition to another aquatic plant termed *Kournabai*, may be a *Triglochia* (?), with a yellow flower and a root considered as a great delicacy. *The Kadolo, or Phascolus rostratus*, is one of our small, creeping, leguminous plants, with three narrow, long, sharp pointed leaves, upon a common stalk, bearing a flower not unlike our cultivated tea, and root compared by Morrill to our carrot, growing abundantly in every plain, valley, or creek bank, and constituting a prominent feature of native gastronomy. The *Banganga*, or *Nargan*, is probably *Caladium macrorhizon* (?) Vent., colonially known as the Creek Lily, with a large poisonous root, employed as a native food, after a peculiar preparation too long for present explanation. The *Ulorin* of Morrill is the small, egg-shaped, slightly acidulated fruit of the *Carissa ovata* of R. Br., and with the previously mentioned *Nargado*, palm-nut or *Cycas media*; the *Taberio*, Leichhardt tree, or *Nauclea leichhardtii* – Fd-Mueller; the native plum, *Owenia cerat sefera* – F.M.; the large pomegranate fruit *Cupparis mitchellii*; the Pink Lily, or *Nelumbium leichhardtii*; two species of Yam, *Dioscorea*; and the *Morgogaba*, native banana, or *Musa jackii*, very abundant round Mount Elliott, and, according to Morrill, extending far inland, constitute the catalogue of plants it has been possible to identify. But at the same time to assist botanical research in the comparatively unknown North-Eastern flora, the aboriginal names of several other plants are appended, including the *Kanoul, Kanana, Boan, Malboun* and *Mogondal*, whose roots or bulbs were employed by the natives as food.

Eric Mjoberg wished to see Aboriginal culture in Australia preserved from advancing civilisation, and wrote letters of concern to the appropriate authorities. He published some of this correspondence in his 1918 book:

To: The Royal Society of New South Wales, Sydney.
Gentlemen.
The conception of "Protection of Nature" has in our days pervaded all civilised countries. The rapid advance of civilisation in all the five continents has threatened to retard or even destroy the original

nature of the country; laws have been proposed and put into effect for the purpose of saving and protecting the same.

It is pleasant to state that in the fifth and youngest of the continents, and perhaps the most interesting of all, where the practical branches have reached a more rapid and radical progress than anywhere in the world, foreseeing men have raised their voices in favour of a rational protection of the rapidly retrogressing original nature of the continent. Subsequently, laws regarding same have been put into effect in all the Australian States.

More severe than anywhere else has the advancing civilisation descended on the aboriginals of the Australian continent. In the southern portion of Queensland, New South Wales, Victoria, the civilised portions of South Australia and West Australia, the aboriginals are almost extinct. Only in the central and the more inaccessible northern portions of the continent do the aboriginals live their true life, although even here the degeneration has plainly spread, threatening them in the near future with a similar fate to that of the aboriginals in the southern now civilised parts. During my two scientific expeditions to Kimberley in the north west and Cape York in the east, I have had exceptional opportunities to personally and at close range convince myself of this fact.

The Governments of the various States must be given credit for their unspared efforts to alleviate the often miserable existence of the already half civilised aboriginals. We must not hesitate to encourage a good deal of mission work, which rightly directed, no doubt

Aborigines with a large battle sword-club, left, and painted rainforest shield. They are standing under a melon-bearing tree, *Carica papaya*, introduced into Australia from overseas, and known locally as "paw paw". Harveys Creek, north Queensland. (Atkinson collection, c. 1890s.)

would be of great help to those aboriginals, which have already been touched by civilisation.

The Australian aboriginal of the stone age, one of the oldest and most interesting races on earth, will, in the near future, be a thing of the past. Only extraordinary and rational measures could save the not yet degenerated remnants from the sad fate of the old Tasmanian aboriginals.

Only on one spot in the vast Queensland, at the Mornington Island on the inner shores of the Gulf of Carpentaria, the aboriginals still live untouched by white civilisation. Presumably a few thousand blacks are there, living the free and undisturbed life of their ancestors, governed by the inner unwritten laws and strict morals, the latter even surpassing those of the whites.

Dr. Roth, who in company of Mr. Hedley, visited the island towards the end of the nineteenth century, describes the inhabitants as healthy and physically well developed people. They did not even know the use of tobacco, a strong proof of that they had not come into contact with the white civilisation. The island which is no less than 35 miles long and at the widest measures 17 miles, is partially covered with Eucalyptus forests and waving grass plains. The island abundantly produces all that those black children of paradise need for their welfare.

It is with great regret that I understand that the authorities intend to civilise this island and that consequently a mission station will be erected there. I do not hesitate to state that this will be the death-blow to the aboriginals of the Island, and within a relative short period the hitherto happy blacks will be changed into the same repellent and pitiable type of native, which one only too often observes in different parts of the continent.

I now ask: Will this be permitted to happen without a warning voice being raised in appeal? Is it not a sacrilege thus to degenerate

1.

2.

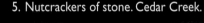

3.

4.

5.

1. Upper and lower grinding stones made from basalt, used to grind vegetable, nut and seed foods. Cedar Creek, north Queensland. Grind stones about 2 feet (60cm) long and one foot (30 cm) wide are kept in every hut. When people move camp, they leave behind the heavy lower stone, but take the top stone with them. After a season, they will return to the area and use the same lower stone again.

2. Giant axe from Malanda, north Queensland.

3. Primitive stone axe from Christmas Creek.

4. Stone, warmed by the blacks and used to treat women's headache. The hot stone is applied to the head.

5. Nutcrackers of stone. Cedar Creek.

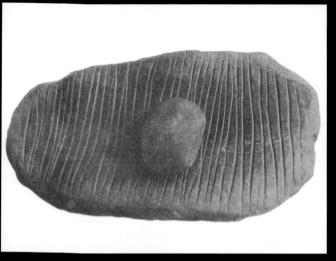

Grindstone, made from slate, with parallel grooves cut into the lower grindstone to keep nuts and other hard material in place, making their grinding easier. Malanda, north Queensland.

1.

2.

3.

. Sharp edged quartzite knife. Cape York Peninsula.

. Sandstone rasp. Coleman River.

. Stone tool with handle from Cape York Peninsula. A piece of vine is bent around the stone head and secured by bees wax or other resin. The base of the loop is kept tight by wrapping with twine and covering with further resin. In this example, only the upper part of the handle is kept together with twine, and the lower part of the handle has sprung apart.